APHORISMS:
FOR THOSE
WHO SEEK THE TRUTH

真
TRVTH

Asitis Now

NowLedge Books

"Peace is not the absence of trials and tribulations, but the absence of doubt and confusion." –Asitis Now

COPYRIGHT

Printed in the United States of America

First Printing, 2013

NowLedge Communications
P.O. Box 613
Morrow, GA 30260

http://nowledgecommunications.webs.com/

asitisnow7@gmail.com

DEDICATION

To my lovely wife, Angela, for being the best and (one of the) wisest choices I have ever made. Thank you for your loyalty, your faithfulness, and your support. Without you, bringing this work to the light may not have ever been made possible. No matter what circumstances may dictate, we shall forever be bonded in the Spirit. You are my soul mate, my partner, my friend, and, I shall always be grateful that my journey of knowledge and truth led me to you.

Love always...

FOREWORD

I was deeply honored when my ex-husband asked me to write the foreword to this his latest work. Having witnessed firsthand his life struggles, his ongoing fight with inner darkness, the rocky path that he has violently traversed, and his own journey to truth, I can attest that this work is the fruit of hard labor, blood, sweat, and tears.

It has long been held a universal truth that strength and great power are birthed out of great adversity. If this is indeed true, then this book is forged in steel.

For millennia mankind has been searching for answers to questions regarding life, death, and his inner self. In these turbulent times, that search has intensified, but no answers seem to be found. A large segment of society continues to struggle with depression, addictions, and a pervading sense of doom on a daily basis as they ponder their self-existence. To fill that inner void people are turning to religion, drugs, alcohol, dysfunctional relationships, food, careers, etc.— anything that will ruffle the time and allow them to escape from their prevalent inner chaotic dissatisfaction; yet, they still wander aimlessly, seeking that which they can't seem to find.

In *Aphorisms: For Those Who Seek the Truth* some of these elusive keys to inner knowledge may be found. Asitis Now comes packing a compendium of knowledge gleaned from his deep studies of scripture, organized religion, philosophy, and

APHORISMS: FOR THOSE WHO SEEK THE TRUTH

life, and attempts to answer those probing questions, or, even better, provide guideposts for the reader to find his own answers. Many universal truths can be found between these covers—good, bad, and ugly.

This is not the type of book that you will pick up, lightly consume, and then return to the bookshelf, never to be seen again. Deep thinkers will devour it as voraciously as a hungry dog consuming a steak, and novice seekers of truth will press forward in fascination towards a dancing fountain of knowledge as they cast aside long held beliefs that have held them captive. As the ideas found within these pages generate answers they also raise other questions and provoke the reader to embark upon a deeper journey of self-enlightenment, reality, and truth.

Prepare your pen, your highlighter, and your journal so that as you begin the contemplative process of self-examination you can capture your interpretations of these nuggets of life in the light of your own personal experiences and find the answers that you seek. You won't be able to say that you weren't forewarned.

Welcome, fellow truth seekers. Prepare to make the trek with us. Your treasure awaits.

-Angela Lane Woods, Author, *Concerning Widowhood: Insights for the Newly Widowed Christian Woman* and *Devotionals for the Brokenhearted*

"Peace is not the absence of trials and tribulations, but the absence of doubt and confusion." –Asitis Now

A WORD FROM THE AUTHOR

This subject matter is written for those who have the courage and the freedom to "think outside of the box."

For all of those who are full of concrete beliefs, fixed opinions, wearying speculations, and complex theories, these writings are not intended for you;

If you fall into the latter category, this book may be utilized as toilet tissue, firewood, or padding for the soft-bottomed.

To those to whom this book is addressed, once you've read all of the pages, <u>forget</u> what it is you have read. This quote from a passage in this book sums it all up: "To cling to words is to embrace definition, and to embrace definition is to set limitations."

These aphorisms are inspired sayings: the many voices of <u>That</u> <u>Which</u> <u>Is</u>. The first person narrative (e.g., I, Me, My, Mine) in this book <u>does</u> <u>not</u> refer to this author, but to that which is infinite and unnameable, what many call "Truth," that ever-evasive concept which changes according to the perception of one's experiences. But even the word <u>Truth</u> is a relative term that alludes to another word which is just as familiar: "False." However, if the word <u>Truth</u> were to be applied in accordance with one of its definitions (dictionary) as "conformity to fact or actuality," there can be no relative term (<u>False</u>), the reason being that <u>that which is not</u> (false) doesn't exist, never did exist, and never will it exist. The word <u>actual</u>, which <u>actuality</u> is derived from, is defined as "Being, existing, or acting at the present moment." So, in essence, <u>Truth</u> is a term associated with <u>The Now</u>, <u>The Present Moment</u>, <u>That Which Is</u>. There is no opposite to existence!

It is highly recommended that you, the reader, acquire your own comprehension from each aphorism; therefore, I, the author, have refrained from adding any commentary. These aphorisms are intended only as a guide to a more in-depth way of looking at Life. <u>Your</u> own real world experiences <u>are</u> <u>your</u> Teacher!

-Asitis Now

"Peace is not the absence of trials and tribulations, but the absence of doubt and confusion." –Asitis Now

INTERNAL WORKS

TABLE OF CONTENTS

APHORISMS: FOR THOSE WHO SEEK THE TRUTH

CHAPTER 1: BOUNDLESS

I can't be found,
I Am Ever-Present.
If I Am sought after,
I become elusive.
Knowledge does not bring Me forth,
And education does not know Me.
Being kind to others,
Nor being mean to others,
Does not alter Me.
I Am what I Am,
And there's no way to define Me.

I Am Infinite and I Am Not.
I have no name nor any attributes,
That can be attributed to Me.
I Am Everything and No Thing.
I Am neither happy nor sad.
There is no feeling to describe Me.
There is no concept to grasp.
The Now is inescapable,
And I flow and flow and flow without cessation.

I Am beyond religion,
And beyond any concept of religion as well.
I Am beyond words and terminologies,
I Am beyond phrases,
And I Am beyond baggage.
To know Me, relinquish all knowledge.
I Am beyond possession.

I Am neither personal nor impersonal.
I don't care nor do I worry.
What is <u>Is</u>.

I Am neither entertaining nor entertained.
I can't be diverted,
Because My course is non-deviating.
I Am unreachable but Ever-Near.

I Am Present when no one's around.
If you look for Me,
You won't see Me.
I Am All-Seeing but never seen.
If you listen for My voice,
You will never hear Me.
I Am All-Hearing but never heard.
If you seek to touch Me,
You won't feel Me.
I Am All-Embracing but never am I embraced.
If you quest to smell My fragrance,
The only smell you smell shall be a stench unto you.
I Am All-Smelling and no smell at all.
If you desire to savor My delicacies,
You will never taste of My nectar.
I Am All-Devouring but never devoured.

I Am beyond descriptions.
I have no color and no measurements.
I Am neither Male nor Female,
Adult nor child.
All things are I and I not all things.

I Am neither separated nor one.

APHORISMS: FOR THOSE WHO SEEK THE TRUTH

Neither divided nor singular.
To call me "One" is to label Me.
To call me "Many" is to label Me.
I Am beyond labels,
For words are only inadequate forms of
      communication.
They are necessary but also unnecessary.
Those who swear by them are bound to them.
Those who believe in words are servants of them.

In order to communicate with Me,
You must become Me.
In order to comprehend Me,
You must liberate yourself of all comprehensions of
      Me.

I have no point-of-view
For within I Am viewless,
And without I Am pointless.
No one can guide you to Me,
Nor can I be guided to you
For I Am without guidance.
To and Fro I go,
While, simultaneously, going nowhere

I Am Ever-Pervading.
Whether you like Me or not,
I still exist.

You will not find Me in a book,
Nor will you find Me on television.
You will not find Me in school,

Nor will you find Me on a Job.
You will not find Me in your companions,
Nor will you find me in your opponents.
There is only one source,
And, if you refuse to look there,
You will overlook Me.

I Am not feelings,
I Am not emotions,
I Am never frustrated,
Because My will is always done.
I Am never disappointed,
Because I don't expect any thing.
I Am never excited,
Because I react to no thing.
I Am never cautious,
Because I Am never afraid.
I Am never hasty,
Because I Am in control of all things.

I Am the cause,
And I Am the effect as well.

I have no preferences,
Because All things are equal to Me,
And All things serve a purpose.

No one group of people retain possession of Me.
I Am not limited to a set of ideals,
Nor will any opinion ratify Me.
I need neither approval nor disapproval to exist.
I Am Self-Existent.
Your movements are My movements,

APHORISMS: FOR THOSE WHO SEEK THE TRUTH

For no thing can happen lest I will it.
When you rail against past, present, and future
        atrocities,
Events and circumstances,
You are in denial of My power.
I Am and will continue to prevail over All things.
Only through Love will you accept My Will.
Only through True Devotion will you truly
        comprehend.

If you seek perfection,
Then, in your mind, you are imperfect.
The natural shedding of concepts,
Such as perfection and imperfection,
Dispel such illusions of defects,
Which are the product of impure thoughts.

My power is unlimited
I speak to those who patiently listen.
I appear to those who are observant.
I Am bitter, and I Am sweet,
But to those who have tasted of My nectar,
I have no distinguishing flavor.
My smell is, both, repulsive and fragrant,
But to those who have experienced My scent,
They perceive no difference.
I Am painful to the touch,
And I Am pleasant to the touch,
But to those who have embraced Me,
I Am beyond any experience of sensation.
I Am Confusion to those,
Who choose to ignore Me.

"Peace is not the absence of trials and tribulations, but the absence of doubt and confusion." —Asitis Now

I Am Complicated to those,
Who choose to analyze Me.
I Am Unpleasant to those,
Who rely on their five physical senses.
I Am Hurt to those,
Who hate painful encounters.
I Am The Past and The Future for those,
Who avoid living in The Present.
I Am Problems to those,
Who view life as difficult.
And I Am Doubt to those,
Who are uncertain of Me.

No thing has influence over Me.
I have no Master.
I make no choices.
Through Me, delusions are,
And, also, through Me delusions are not.
Those who are deluded reject Me,
And those who are no longer deluded,
Recognize Me as I Am.

I Am neither "right" nor "wrong."
Remove the veil of languages,
And you will notice Me.
I Am closer to you than you imagine.
In fact, if you no longer rely on your imagination,
There I Am.

Many say they believe in miracles,
But when I Am revealed to them,
They dis-believe Me.
Many say they have faith,

APHORISMS: FOR THOSE WHO SEEK THE TRUTH

But when faced with adversities,
They question Me.
Many say they love and cherish Me,
But when I speak to them,
They run away from Me.
Many say they have hopes and dreams,
But when I shatter them,
They wonder why.

There are many who say they "know" Me,
But I Am intimate only with those,
Who abandon their knowledge.
There are many who say they seek Me,
But I Am manifested only to those,
Who abandon their search.
There are many who attempt to sway others,
Towards their concept of Me,
But I Am inconceivable only to those,
Who abandon their ideas.

To those who are arrogant
I appear to them as self-important,
But when they unite with Me,
No thing is more important than an "other."

I Am Experience and I Am, also Non-experience.
I Am that which you see,
And I Am, equally, that which you don't see.
Whether you do or don't,
I Am doing and I Am not doing.

I Am "crazy" to those,

Who consider themselves "sane,"
And I Am "sane" to those,
Who others call "crazy."

Little children honor Me,
With their actions and their speech.
When they are in need,
Their parents are made aware.

When a little child,
Hears the word "hot" for the first time,
The word is empty and meaningless.
But when that same little child,
Touches a "hot" stove,
I Am Fully Realized!

I Am within you,
And you are within Me.
We are One.
Not in the numerical sense,
But in its universality—its Non-Duality.
When you awaken from your dream-world,
You'll see me as I Am.

You and your divisions,
Are the creator of confidence and doubt.
You and your divisions,
Are the creator of "good" and "evil."
You and your divisions,
Are the creator of courage and fear.
You and your divisions,
Are the creator of love and hate.
You and your divisions,

APHORISMS: FOR THOSE WHO SEEK THE TRUTH

Are the creator of likes and dislikes.
You and your divisions,
Are the creator of attraction and aversions.
You and your divisions,
Are the creator of beauty and ugly.
You and your divisions,
Are the creator of superior and inferior.
You and your divisions,
Are the creator of harmony and disharmony.
You and your divisions,
Are the creator of one race and an "other" race.
And all other divisions,
Are the product of your divided mentality.
When you desist from your reactive thinking,
Then you will realize that I Am not divided.
I Am "Creator" to those,
Who see "themselves" as separate from Me.
I Am neither creator nor creation to those,
Who see me every-where and no-where.

Whether you believe in Me, or not,
You are bound to Me.
Whether you choose to face Me, or not,
You are bound to Me.
But, fret not, for even in your bondage to Me,
You are free and boundless.

CHAPTER 2: THE BODY OF REALITY

If you identify <u>only</u> with the physical body,
You are not in harmony with Me.
I Am within all containers,
But never am I to be contained.

I Am the Teacher within.
I Am that internal process.
I Am that which motivates.
To embrace Me,
Stop identifying <u>only</u> with the physical body.

Devote yourself to Me,
And your search ends.
I will free you of all delusions.
With Me, there is no "either/or,"
Only that which <u>is</u>.

Regardless of your geographical location,
My Will operates unbiasedly.
<u>Being</u> is what I Am,
And I Am without rest or cessation.

Being impatient,
Will not cause Me to act nor react.
I Am Action and Reaction.
I Am the Cause of your impatience,
And I Am, also, the effect of your impatience.
I Am that which you consider problems,
And I Am, also, the solution to your problems.
Face Me and you will see Me.
If you look anywhere else but directly at Me,

APHORISMS: FOR THOSE WHO SEEK THE TRUTH

You will continue to be delusional.

Why do you attempt to "beautify,"
That which is already beautiful?
Why do you want to "perfect,"
That which is already perfect?
Why do you wish to "complete,"
That which is already complete?
Why do you desire to "make whole,"
That which is already whole?
You have allowed the unappeasable fire of desire,
Which is illusion to permeate your being.
You have allowed your Judgment,
To be distorted by mirrors.
In order to see things as they really are,
You must look within.

When you are swayed by "outside" influences,
You enter the realm of opinions.
And when you settle in that realm,
You are far from Me.

I Am intimate with those,
Who are intimate with themselves.
Those who go on an "inner journey,"
Experience Me in every thing,
In every one, and every way.

Just as the organs in the body perform different
        functions,
But serve a common purpose to keep it, the body
        alive,

"Peace is not the absence of trials and tribulations, but the absence of doubt and confusion." –Asitis Now

So do I in the universal body perform various deeds,
For I Am the Controller of All functions.

One does not make "mistakes,"
One only has experiences.
And, in these experiences,
One comes face to face with Me.

The chain of events,
That have led you to this point,
Are all various aspects of Me.
You can choose to face Me,
Or turn away from Me.
Regardless of your choices,
I Am still present.

What you consider "mistakes" or "bad choices,"
Are nothing but meaningless words,
For they have no bearing on Me.

When a glass of milk,
Is spilled on the floor,
The action cannot be un-done.
The only deed to perform,
Is to use a rag or paper towel to wipe up the spill.
Then, once you have performed that task,
Pour yourself another glass of milk.
Don't berate yourself over a past experience.

To replay images in your mind of past experiences,
Is akin to adding more water to a glass already full.
Your only success will be in creating a puddle.

APHORISMS: FOR THOSE WHO SEEK THE TRUTH

In every encounter I Am there.
There are no co-incidences.
To live is to be conscious of Me in every thing.
You can not evade Me.
In your mind you may think you can hide from Me,
But deep within your being you know Me.

When one identifies only with the physical body,
One believes it can be beautified with clothes,
Makeup, jewelry, "nip-tucks," hairstyles, exercise,
And facial creams.
In this every effort to "beautify,"
One, <u>unconsciously</u>, is saying "I am not beautiful
            enough."
The need to feel beautiful makes you <u>un-beautiful</u>!
Knowledge of Me eliminates "the need."

When one identifies with only the physical body,
One is easily influenced by slogans.
When one identifies with the universal body,
One <u>Is</u> the Influence!

Because one believes they are separate from Me,
I Am the source of all illusions.
Unite with Me and dispel such notions.

Too much thought brings about too much regret,
Thus the mind tends to overlook Me.
When one focuses on the eternal "I,"
One has no regret or remorse.
One who has attained the highest reality,
Is one who has accepted Me as I Am.

One who operates only on the physical plane,
Is one who is guided by the sense-pleasures.
What you see is what you get.

I Am Fear-of-Death,
To those who cling to life.
I Am Fear-of-Failure,
To those who cling to success.
I Am Fear-of-Rejection,
To those who cling to acceptance.
I Am Fear-of-Loss,
To those who cling to possessions.
I Am Fear-of-Ridicule,
To those who cling to opinions.
I Am Fear-of-Under-achievement,
To those who cling to ambition.
I Am Fear-of-Pain,
To those who cling to pleasure.
I AM Fear-of-Unfulfillment,
To those who cling to hope.
I Am Fear-of-Reality,
To those who cling to beliefs.

Those who hate simplicity, hate Me.
Those who seek challenges want explanations.
Your words and I are not intimate,
They only strengthen ignorance.
Leave off speaking and there I.
Your perceptions and I are not intimate,
They only strengthen delusions.
Leave off observations and there I.
You see, <u>not-knowing</u> and I are most intimate.

APHORISMS: FOR THOSE WHO SEEK THE TRUTH

Your memories separate you from Me,
For they are but rote ideas of the past.
I Am Spontaneous.
I Am Now.
I Am Unpredictable.

When seeking self-improvement,
Your mind is under the influence of opinions.
Do you feel you are too fat? Too skinny?
Do you wish you were taller? Shorter?
What, or who, are you using as a gauge?
When you realize that you are Pure Being,
These word comparisons become meaningless.
Action is Existence and Existence is Motion.

Words are empty.
When spoken, they are borne upon hot wind,
And they disperse among the clouds.
One who is not hung up on words,
Is like a bird which flies south during the winter,
Leaving no trace of the route in which it has flown.

To the un-enlightened mind,
Words have a powerful influence,
But to one who has achieved illumination,
Words are not worthy of analyzation.

One who sees flaws in his physical body,
Is full of flaws in the mind.
One who notices imperfections in others,
Has no intimacy with perfection themselves.
Just as perfection can not bring forth imperfection,

"Peace is not the absence of trials and tribulations, but the absence of doubt and confusion." –Asitis Now

Neither can imperfection produce perfection.
That which is <u>Is</u>.

When you identify only with the physical body
You are a servant of Me.
When you identify with the soul,
You are a part of Me.
But, when you identify with the Self,
You <u>are</u> Me!

Those who limit themselves,
Limit their access to Me.

Storing up gossip about "others" in your mind,
Is as useless as saving toilet tissue,
Stained with human feces.

In ignorance one sees only the branches,
But one who embraces Me notices the root.

Ideas, concepts, images, thoughts, and sensations,
Are the branches which change,
But, the root, change not.
I existed before the branches,
And I will exist when they are gone.

Stop trying to find your self,
And Just Be!
If you rely on that which is impermanent,
You will be disappointed.
Change is inevitable.
Don't resist it or cling to it.
Just as the change of seasons reflect My Laws,

APHORISMS: FOR THOSE WHO SEEK THE TRUTH

One thought gives rise to an other.
The wise feels neither attraction nor aversions,
Nor mixed emotions regarding their thoughts.
They let them flow together naturally.

If you suffer from boredom,
It is because you are thinking "mind uninteresting."
Transcend the need for entertainment and escape,
And you will see that the inner realm is equally
        fascinating.

All Beings as they are are Me.
Trying to become this,
Or trying to become that,
Is the conditioning of a deluded mind.
The Purified Mind is free from such delusions.

What you are now is all that matters.
Stop imagining your self as imperfect.
There is neither nor,
Only that which Is.
Accept Me and you accept you.

When you enter into the full knowledge of Me,
You will realize that you know nothing at all.

The Mind is unlimited.
The more you learn,
The more you are capable of learning.
Like a sponge,
It soaks up all it comes into contact with.
The moment you conclude that you know nothing,

Is the instant you know All.

The mind, like the mirror,
Is able to reflect whatever image comes before it.
As long as one doesn't cling to reflections,
There's always room for more images.

All are subject to My Laws,
There is no one or no thing exempt.

When one is impatient and in a rush,
One is bound to the future.
The only reality, that which is actual, is Now.
Those looking toward the future avoid Me,
But those who are patient truly live.

By living in the Present,
And accepting present conditions,
Neither in attachment nor aversion,
One realizes the True Gift of Life,
And is one with the Body of Reality.

CHAPTER 3: DUSTY MIRROR

I t is hard to glimpse one's reflection in a dusty
mirror.
The image will be distorted.
And one's view in the mirror is impeded.

Like the dusty mirror,
When the mind is impure with beliefs, concepts,
and ideals,
One sees only a partial view,
Rather than the entire picture.

If you have a concept of Me,
It's as if you're chasing the wind.
Just as one cannot catch the wind,
One will never get wind of Me.

I Am Ever-Elusive,
To those who chase after Me.
As long as one imagines Me,
To be "this" or "that,"
I Am the Producer of False Views.

If one wishes to see themselves clearly in the
mirror,
One must wipe away the dust.
To see Me as I Am,
One must wipe out all beliefs.

If one were to disregard a dusty mirror,

Seeking to find a clean mirror,
One would be distracted.
It would be easier to just clean the mirror in front of
them.
The distracted mind doesn't comprehend this, of
course.
Rather than removing the dust, the beliefs one
possesses,
One would rather seek "cleanliness" elsewhere,
Thus be in constant distraction.

Thoughts are inconstant,
So why cling to them?

Not only does knowledge separate,
But one becomes firm in this knowledge, thus solid,
un-movable.
In order to transcend knowledge and achieve
liberation,
One must become like water that flows and
penetrates.

If you want to know Me,
Stop lying to your self.

When you lie to other people,
You are in denial of Me.
You are what you are.
What else can you be?

When you submit to being,

You live in Me and I in you.

APHORISMS: FOR THOSE WHO SEEK THE TRUTH

When you lie to make your self seem more
		important,
You are unconsciously,
Saying you are not satisfied with your present
		status.

To an enlightened being,
Lies are like dust on a mirror.
And the enlightened one uses a damp wet cloth
		called Reality,
Because one has the power to look beyond the
		dust, the lies,
And know that the mirror is perfect.

When one's mind is always "thinking ahead,"
One never enjoys the moment.

Those who meditate on Me,
Meditate on nothing.
A clear mind,
Like a clear mirror,
Allows one to see much.

Those who are aware of their thoughts and emotions,
As they arise within,
Are those who are awake and not asleep.
Just as when one is physically sleeping,
One is not aware of the "outer world," mentally,
Those who are mentally asleep,
Are not aware of the "inner world," physically.
When one awakens to Me,
One sees the "inner" and "outer world" in its

non-duality,
And comes to the realization there is no difference.

When one is being,
One dis-covers.
When one is trying to be,
One is dis-eased.

Particles of dust are always floating around in a
   room,
But it takes the sunbeam, shining through the
   window,
To illuminate them to the naked eye.
Thus the room is always in need of a constant
   dusting and cleaning.
Likewise, all types of thoughts and desires flow
   constantly in the mind,
But it takes awareness to not be compelled by
   them,
Thus the mind is always in need of personal
   attention.

With Me, there is no "inner" nor "outer world."
One who is intimate with Me makes no such
   distinction.

The wind has no fixed abode;
Neither do I.

In Me, there is no thing to learn.
Once one relinquishes the desire to learn,
One has attained All.
There is no thing to learn,

APHORISMS: FOR THOSE WHO SEEK THE TRUTH

When one embraces Me as I Am.

When one desires,
One lives in fantasy,
And overlooks that which is.
When one has hopes,
One is expectant.
And when one is expectant,
One is bound to be disappointed.

Those who are conscious of the Now,
Are like cleaning services ever-cleaning.

If you have time to point your finger at "an other,"
You are not utilizing your time properly.
The experiences of "an other,"
Are not your experiences.
You are Here right Now!
Where they've been is not your reality.

I Am Peace,
To those who bask in the present moment.
If you believe you have to achieve something,
In order to be at peace,
You'll be waiting indefinitely.

Like a mother full of unconditional love,
For all of her offsprings,
I do not "take sides" or induce separation.
My Laws fall equally upon all creation.
When you hate "an other,"
You hate your self,

And when you hate your self,
You hate Me.
But if you love Me,
You'll love your self,
Thus you'll comprehend "an other,"
And it all transforms into Pure Love.

The make-up of people,
Consists of their experiences.
In order to know them,
You must cease believing you are any different.

Unless one takes the same journey,
One can not know the outcome.
The enlightened being knows this,
And ceases to speculate and be judgmental.

A mirror that is neglected,
Is apt to collect dust.
A mind that is ignored,
Is apt to accumulate beliefs, concepts, and ideals.

Those who concentrate on the affairs of "an other,"
Neglect the affairs of their own mind.

A neglected mind is easily swayed by influences.
A neglected mind is easily swayed by "experts."
A neglected mind is easily swayed by circumstances.
A neglected mind is easily swayed by conditions.
A neglected mind is easily swayed by opinions.
A neglected mind is easily swayed by doctrines.
A neglected mind is easily swayed by culture.
A neglected mind is easily swayed by the majority.

APHORISMS: FOR THOSE WHO SEEK THE TRUTH

A neglected mind is easily swayed by beliefs.
A neglected mind is easily swayed by words.
A neglected mind is easily swayed by speculations.
A neglected mind is easily swayed by rumors.

Many say they believe in past miracles,
Such as "walking on water" or "parting the Red
      Sea,"
But when informed of <u>their</u> own power of
      perfection and contentment,
They are full of disbelief and doubt.

A neglected mind is easily swayed by "<u>His</u>tory."
The well-tended mind uncovers My Story in
      mystery.

Moment by moment I speak volumes,
To those who care to listen.
I Am Most Exquisite,
To those who hunger for Me.
Though many find Me Distasteful,
I Am Most Satisfying,
To those who delight in Me.
Just as one, who is satiated, walks away from a
      table filled with food,
So it is with one who has found contentment with
      Me,
And walks away from knowledge.

When a dusty mirror is cleansed
One need not know what is behind the dust.
So it is with the cleansed mind,

One need not know why one has beliefs, concepts,
        and ideals.
Whether a mirror is clean, or not,
It is still a mirror.
So it is with the mind.
The power is ever-present to bring forth all things.

Those who settle in comfort,
Are in direct opposition to the natural law of
        change.

Those who are filled with vanity,
Are enamored by their own image in the mirror.
Thus they spend a lot of time in front of one.
So it is with the fact-gatherers,
Who are enraptured by knowledge retained in their
        minds.
Thus they become inflexible and arrogant in their
        beliefs.

The movement is in the moment.
All else is non-existent.
The so-called "past" has passed on,
Thus, it is <u>non-existent</u>.
The so-called "future" is yet-to-be, fictitious, prospective,
However, still, <u>non-existent</u>.
This moment, this instant, though, is alive.
You can't redo, or udo, that which is already done,
Nor can you predict the <u>exact</u> path you'll travel.

You only have control over your movement, this
        moment,
The only true influential power you possess.

34

APHORISMS: FOR THOSE WHO SEEK THE TRUTH

When one has contempt for "an other,"
One despises that which is,
And misses the opportunity for enlightenment.

Where is My dwelling place?
Where do I reside?
Those who ask these questions,
Spend an awful lot of time thinking,
And are as the narcissists
Who love their mirrored image.

Those who cherish their thoughts,
Love not Me.
While a thought is but fleeting,
I Am Eternal.

One's perspective changes with influence,
Just as uprooted flowers blow to and fro in the
        wind.
But those who are unmoved by thoughts,
Remain upright as a tall oak tree rooted in the
        earth.

Those who know where they are heading in life,
Are those who know nothing at all.
Those who know not their direction in life,
Are those who know all.
Thus their options remain open and flexible.

Those who dwell in Me,
Dwell in the moment.

Those who dwell in the past,
Are afraid of the never-ending challenges of the New.
Those who dwell in the future,
Are forever reaching.

Those who judge upon the outer appearance,
Are like one who comes across a dusty mirror,
And dismiss it as "junk."
Those who are in harmony with Me,
Realize that the mirror is capable of being cleansed,
And, thus, utilized.

The deluded one,
Who has been doing a thing incorrectly for a long
        time,
While under the impression that it is correct,
Despises correction from an outer source.

Remove the dust from the mirror,
And you'll see your reflection more clearly.
Remove beliefs, concepts, desires, and ideals from
        your mind,
And you'll appreciate life as it is.

CHAPTER 4: THE ETERNAL CASCADE

I do not sleep nor eat.
I Am in motion constantly like a cascade,
Descending upon steep rocks while replenishing the
water below.

To those accustomed to Me,
I Am welcomed in any form.
My presence is accepted on all terms.

You can't hide from Me,
Nor can you hide within Me.
Wherever you go, I Am There.

I Am –Ever-Vocal concerning all deeds.
Whether "good" or "bad,"
You shall hear Me speak.

Many in their avoidance of Me,
Confuse their desires with needs.
Those truly in need are not "picky."

Those who seek to learn Me,
Know nothing about the process of learning.
One need only to live, freely, without preconceived
notion.
This, even a newborn infant knows.

A <u>True</u> act of love,
May, sometimes, appear harsh and selfish.
But, for those who search within,
Many lessons are gleaned.

Misfortunes come,
And misfortunes go.
One who accepts this fact,
Is one who is truly unaffected.

One who grumbles and grumbles,
But never brings forth a change,
Is like one who masturbates and masturbates,
But never brings forth new life.

Why are you searching for Me?
I Am not lost.
Disintegrate your beliefs,
And you'll see Me as Being.

I Am the seasons that change.
I Am the snow that falls and turns into sleet and ice.
I Am the rain that becomes hail and snow.
I Am all that is impermanent.

I Am beyond slogans and catchwords.
You can't make Me up.
I already exist.

By directing your journey every where else but within,
You miss out on the opportunity to know the
        greatest mystery.
What happens after you are physically dead is

unimportant.
What is important is what happens to you now.
Anything beyond that is speculation or belief.

A diamond is no more expensive than a rock.
It is the individual who places different values upon
    them.
They both serve their purposes.
If one wants to build a house with stones,
Chances are, a diamond would not be first choice.

Words are dependent upon one's interpretation of
    them.
Leave off speaking much, and let action do the
    justifying.

Those who choose comfort over hardship,
Neglect challenging the mind.
But those who treat both comfort and hardship
    equally,
Are forever accepting new challenges.

"Blessings" and "cursings" originate from the same
    source,
So why not accept them un-equivocally?

I Am the Author of all manifestations.
How one sees them depends on one's relationship
    with Me.
No thing changes because one thinks otherwise.
The "you" that exists now,
Is an offspring of all your experiences.

Being is the true ruler of all,
Not the mind.
When one is a servant of the wind,
One is enslaved by the desires of the mind.

One's mind is framed by one's experiences,
And the mind forms opinions, beliefs, and concepts,
        based on these experiences.
But one who is immersed in Being, simply, accepts
        all experiences,
As the way of life without differentiating.
Thus one is free to "Be."

That, which is falsehood, an illusion,
Is blown away life chaff in the wind.
But, that which is of Me, The Reality,
Is planted firm and steadfast.

The cascade is Being without cessation.
So it is with those who are immersed in Me.
And those who are submerged in Me,
See the temporary as "chaff in the wind,"
And the eternal as that which "is planted firm and
        steadfast."
So, why cling to that which is easily stripped away?

So called "physical beauty" is a matter of opinion,
And opinions are not real or concrete.
Besides, "physical beauty" is subject to change,
        destruction, and decay.
So, why cling to that which is easily stripped away?
If one is looking for answers in "an other,"

APHORISMS: FOR THOSE WHO SEEK THE TRUTH

One will never find it,
Because Being is the only answer.
Those who embark on an inner journey experience
    this reality.

No one can guide "you" to Me.
One who embraces the moment knows where I Am.

When one displays anger at "an other,"
It is due to unfulfilled desire in oneself.

Weakness displayed by one,
Is not the product of a weak mind.
It is an extension of one's failure to recognize the
    power
Of one's mind and thus one's failure to cultivate
    said mind.

Beliefs are irrelevant to the wise.
It is experience that truly brings about
    enlightenment.

One who clings to beliefs is one easily led astray,
But, one who embraces the moment, is one on a
    journey.

Trying to understand "an other" is a wayward
    exercise.
Constant Being in the moment,
And adapting to it,
Is creativity at its finest.

Those who are constantly "forced" to react,
Are a product of their environmental influence.
Whereas, those who "choose" to be pro-active,
Influence their environment.

Those who dislike "an other,"
Based on the latter's verbalization,
Are reactors rather than pro-actors,
And thus inhospitable towards that which is.

<u>Right</u> <u>Now</u> one has to deal with Right Now;
The only constant.

The energy wasted on criticizing "an other,"
Is better utilized internally.

No one or no thing is free of Me.
All are subject to My laws.
Whether one "believes" or "disbelieves" is
        irrelevant,
For All are dependent upon Me.

One can conjure up many different images in one's
        mind,
But they are not manifested until one actualizes
        them.

Spiritual life begins ...
When one no longer sees oneself as separate.

The best way to avoid Me,
Is to seek Me.

APHORISMS: FOR THOSE WHO SEEK THE TRUTH

Like the wind, one can feel its presence without
        seeing it.
One can also see the manifestation of its power ...
Without feeling it;
Am I any different?

The most logical conclusion is <u>no</u> conclusion.

The only pure state is that which is.

Stop "becoming" and experience Being!

In "sorrow" one knows who truly is "a friend."

One who is in constant pursuit of happiness,
Is one who will never know true happiness.

True happiness is eternal, never-ending.
That, which is temporary, is only passing,
Thus only an illusion.

When one is acceptant of life as it is,
One is truly happy with one's life <u>as it is</u>.

There is no such entity as "in-dependent,"
For all are interdependent.

In order for one to act,
One must inter-act.
I Am Development in the present tense.
I Am the Nature of all creation.

One whose sole focus is development of the
        physical,
Is one who is dead to Me and misguided.
The power to develop consciously exists within, <u>not</u>
        without.

So-called "mankind" develops according to the
        seeds of consciousness,
That are planted within the mind.
That, which is most conscious—<u>alive</u> to "mankind,"
        Is most controlling to "mankind."

The senses are limited.
In order for the senses to transmit information to
        the mind,
The senses must come into contact with some
        object or sensation.
One needs light to be able to see something in
        darkness,
And one needs a microscope in order to see
        something microscopic.
Thus, the senses are limited.
Why rely on that which is limited?

Driven by desires,
One is enslaved.

One who seeks to possess any thing,
Is one who is possessed.

For every cascading thought that arises,
There is an influence even more powerful.
When one becomes influential rather than

influenced,
One is truly being.

What is mistaken for "love" in the material world,
Is only lust, or desire for personal sense
        gratification.

Outside of loving Me,
There is no possibility of loving.

So-called "love" in the material world,
Means that "you gratify my senses, I'll gratify
        yours."
As soon as the gratification stops,
Immediately there is divorce, separation, quarrel,
        and hatred.

When one is excited over the "attention" from " an
        other,"
One is under the influence of sense gratification.

All one has to do is <u>live</u>,
See one's experiences as they are,
Thus the <u>veil</u> is re-moved.

As water is forgotten as a necessity,
Once one's thirst is satiated,
I am equally neglected.
As food is forgotten as a necessity,
Once one's hunger is satiated,
I Am equally neglected.
As the air one breaths is forgotten as a necessity,

Once one's lungs are filled,
I Am equally neglected.
As the evacuation of bowels is forgotten as a
        necessity,
Once one's defecation is complete,
I Am equally neglected.
As the emptying of the bladder is forgotten as a
        necessity,
Once one's urinary functions are complete,
I Am equally neglected.

Those who believe that luxuries are necessary,
Are those who have truly forgotten their priorities.

CHAPTER 5: UNBELIEVING BELIEF

The very idea of belief implies a residue of doubt,
But <u>knowing</u> leaves no trace of skepticism.
It means certainty. Complete conviction. In your gut.
In your heart. In your soul.

In order to know what comes next,
The veil must be re-moved.

Know this to be the highest aspect of Me:
All creation is Reality.
There's a blessing in <u>every</u> lesson from "Every One" and
    "Every Thing."

One who mocks is one who believes,
But one who knows has no beliefs.

One's "unbelief" is based upon "an other's belief,"
Though neither one can prove the other incorrect.

One of the great realities and equalities:
The moment one is born,
Whether in a crack house or the White House,
One has no idea when or how death will come.

One of the great realities and equalities:
One has no idea who or what,
The most important influences of our lives will be.
One who embraces the Now has truly won.

The most important task,
Is that task being undertaken at that very moment.
And the most important person,
Is that person in your presence at that very moment.

The Now is all one has.
There's no "later" to be possessed or had.

If one does good <u>Now</u>,
One <u>is</u> good.

One who stops loving things and using people,
And turns around and starts loving people and using things,
Is one who knows true freedom.

One need not travel the world over,
In order to find Me.
I Am the Path of Life,
That constant awakening.
All must travel this road.
I Am, simply, <u>Being</u>.

Things are neither perfect nor imperfect,
They are what they are.
Every thing has absolute worth,
Hence nothing can be compared with any thing else.

Two words: Reality changes!

The only thing constant is change!

Your possibilities are greater than your attainments,

48

APHORISMS: FOR THOSE WHO SEEK THE TRUTH

However ... there are greater attainments to come.

Those who have eyes for symbolism see clearly.

The gates of life are but a stage,
The distance between stopping points on a journey.

The masses are pregnant with ambition,
But no one wants to give birth,
Thereby ending the pregnancy.

Duration of thought,
Is composed of instants superior to "time."

Life is uncertain!
Death is certain!
Those who dwell on the past abhor uncertainty.
They walk—unchallenged—among the dead.

A journey to many places if fruitless,
If one knows not the true nature of all creation.

Peace is not attained by "giving up the world,"
Or withdrawing from all relationships or situations;
Peace is achieved by learning to operate your life,
In accordance with Me—the universal law.

There is no difference between a child and adult;
What bridges the gap between the two is experience.

Reflection is seeing Me in "yourself."
Realization is being and actualizing Me.

"Peace is not the absence of trials and tribulations, but the absence of doubt and confusion." –Asitis Now

When one child is born,
One child is <u>fine</u>.
Then one child becomes <u>de-fined</u>.
Thus, one adult must be <u>re-fined</u>.

Beliefs are from without;
Knowledge is from within.
One knows what one knows because one knows,
And it has nothing to do with "others'" opinions or world
        views.

One must forget what one has been taught,
So that one can remember what one knows.

If fear was real,
Everyone would be afraid of the same things.

One must delve into the core of being,
To find that thing which is most sacred: Life.

Since Life is integral,
No single aspect can be held as "unholy."

Just as an undeveloped fetus is lifeless,
One who doesn't develop is dead.

Two words: Cherish being.

If fear is dominant in your life,
It is your "god."
If frustration is dominant in your life,
It is your "god."
If lust is dominant in your life,

APHORISMS: FOR THOSE WHO SEEK THE TRUTH

It is your "god."
If misery is dominant in your life,
It is your "god."
If beliefs are dominant in your life,
They are your "gods."
If desire is dominant in your life,
It is your "god."

That which issues from you is magnetism,
Make yours beneficial unto you,
For you are the magnet which attracts both woes and
        wonders.
Your magnetism influences others in their dealings with
        you

One is enslaved by one's appetite.

One who seeks outer authorities to answer inner issues,
Is one who runs swiftly away from Me.

If you're not using your mind, who is?

Most choose to follow the masses,
Rather than their own thoughts.

Those who raise their heads above the herds,
See the broader horizon.

Where there is enmity,
I Am not.
Where there is bickering,
I Am not.

"Peace is not the absence of trials and tribulations, but the absence of doubt and confusion." –Asitis Now

One who knows Me,
Need not fight in defense of Me.
One who embraces Me,
Need not argue in favor of Me.

Where there is resistance to change,
I Am not.
Where there is imbalance,
I Am not.
Where there is subjectivity,
I Am not.

Food in, waste out.
Knowledge in, belief out.
Water in, urine out.
Wisdom in, ignorance out.

Nature gives and receives,
But those who are ignorant of their own nature,
Desire the role of recipient.

"Time" is an illusion,
For there is nothing fixed:
Change is the only constant!

Peace is not the absence of struggle,
But the absence of doubt and confusion.

Love resides within.
When was the last time you paid a visit there?
When one believes they are right,
Who are you to convince them otherwise?

APHORISMS: FOR THOSE WHO SEEK THE TRUTH

Experience replaces belief,
Therefore knowledge is born.

True teaching is learning simultaneously.

The realm of creating is Heaven,
And the realm of reacting is Earth.
The Earth is a manifestation of that which is in Heaven,
And the Heaven has dominion over the Earth.
Therefore one must be constantly mindful of the Heavenly
        realm.
In order to manifest control over the Earthly realm.

If one places one's hands or feet upon the surface of water,
The water—though touched—retains no hand or
        footprints.
So it is with one whose focus is upon the moment.
The moment—though experienced—is erased by another
        moment.

If every car stopped in a tunnel instead of passing through,
The tunnel would become congested.
If one became attached to things that pass through one's
        life,
One's mind would become transfixed.
One in union with Me is receptive and keeps moving;
One does not stop one's growth for the sake of comfort.
One does not cling to ideals.

One teaches not by words but by being.
One can not "run" from one's self.

"Peace is not the absence of trials and tribulations, but the absence of doubt and confusion." —Asitis Now

Quick Metamorphosis: Bring Me to one who is ignorant of
        Me,
And watch the immediate transformation from "beauty" to
        "beast."

Predictability brings about pushability.

Most do not desire Me,
For they love to cling to beliefs.
And that which consists of beliefs,
Is antithetical to Me.

One who has an unbelieving belief is unmovable,
But one who sustains <u>no</u> knowledge changes.

One without discipline is one without integrity.

A life unexamined is not a life lived.

Decisions are made in darkness,
But actions are manifested in the breaking of day.

Negative existence is comparable to an idea;
It is simultaneously hidden and existent but without
        definition.
Positive existence is parallel to action;
It is concurrently manifested and existent and capable of
        definition.
The action could not exist without an idea.
The earth is alive.
If one wants to know how sacred water is,
Go without it for four days.
One's gratitude for the gift of water returns with that first

APHORISMS: FOR THOSE WHO SEEK THE TRUTH

sip.

An idea is a seed planted in the womb—the mind;
There it is nurtured and it develops,
Later giving birth to action.

It is one's beliefs that oppress one's self.

If <u>it</u> can be explained and in precise detail,
<u>It</u> has nothing to do with Me.
If <u>it</u> can be expressed in language,
<u>It</u> has nothing to do with Me.
To know a cow is to experience a cow,
Not read about one.
A dictionary says nothing about its smell.

The source of language is experience.

One who keeps innerly silent touches the roots of speech.

"In the beginning was the word."
Before that was silence.

Action is clearly manifested,
But one's belief is questionable.

There's more power in silence than in speech.

CHAPTER 6: THE PERFECT SEED

Perfection is not the way things <u>should</u> be,
But the way things actually <u>are</u>.
Perfection is never finished—never complete,
But always growing,
Like a perfect seed growing into a perfect flower.
<u>Not</u> from "imperfection" to Perfection,
But from Perfection to Perfection.

All creation is good.
"Bad" is how many see those experiences,
That play a part in the growth,
One does not yet understand.

The greatest classroom in this universe is within.

In learning one does not take vacations.

Every thing and every one are servants.
All creation serves Being.
This is Perfection.

There are no "bad" experiences.
All experiences serve the growth of one.

One is most happy when one is truthful with one's self.

Those who point out "imperfections" in "others,"
Believe in the greatest myth of all.

Beliefs don't teach,
Experience does.

APHORISMS: FOR THOSE WHO SEEK THE TRUTH

Many attempt to "humanize" others,
So that they won't feel alone in their beliefs of
      "imperfections."
But one who has truly elevated above those types of
      distinctions,
Sees nothing wrong with life as it is.

One need not further define <u>experience</u>,
By qualifying it with adjectives such as "good" or "bad."
Experiences are what they are.
And for one who is conscious of this reality
They are part of the overall development process.

To study means to investigate.
If one has not fully exhausted <u>all</u> possibilities,
<u>And</u> systematically observed <u>all</u> data,
Then one's investigation is incomplete.

Relying <u>totally</u> on "an other's" experience,
Is like utilizing their answers in a test.
In the end you are only cheating.

Only an incompetent makes assumptions before
      completion.

One's body is nourished by food,
And one's being is nurtured by teaching and experience.

Just as a flower needs both the sun and the rain to grow,
So does joy and pain necessitate the development of being.
When one is conscious of the way life is,

"Peace is not the absence of trials and tribulations, but the absence of doubt and confusion." –Asitis Now

And embraces the Now moment by moment,
One is full of peace.

Spontaneity brings into being creativity.

Just as one who is blind,
Is able to navigate one's way in darkness,
So it is with one who is Perfect.
One adapts to the circumstance without complaint.

One who believes in "imperfections,"
Is the one who is truly mentally-challenged.

One who wishes to avoid hardships,
Is one who doesn't know the natural process of a perfect
        seed.

If the seed is perfect,
Should not that which springs forth from it also be perfect?

Those who identify with the "flesh" only,
See only the "self" in mirrored images.

To "disagree" is to renounce the safe and easy path of
        flattery.

Words that lure you,
Rule you.

One who desires the answer,
Before experiencing the question,
Is one who is intimate with categories.

APHORISMS: FOR THOSE WHO SEEK THE TRUTH

Don't categorize!
Look for the wholeness in All.

What one is doing now,
Is what one is doing now.
Though there be many possibilities,
Only one is actually factually.

Whatever one is doing now,
Is in perfect harmony with purpose.

There is no alternative to that which is.

I Am the Perfect Seed which grows myriad.

The ignorant are dead before they die,
While the awakened ones are resurrected from the dead.

One's life is a mirror of the dominant thoughts one thinks.

When one imagines another alternative,
To what is happening at the moment,
One is entertaining illusions.

The realm of visualization is real.
It is the field where everything is created.
And the physical is just the result of the real field of all
        creation.

All actions are preceded by thoughts,
And all thoughts are preceded by being.

All thoughts and ideas,
Whether "positive" or "negative,"
Constitute the perfect seed.
They are the cause of all actions.

All actions,
Whether "positive" or "negative,"
Constitute the perfect fruit.
They are in perfect harmony with the thoughts that
        precede them.

When one realizes that all one's actions are perfect,
Whether "positive" or "negative,"
And are the product of one's thoughts,
Which are also perfect,
Then one becomes conscious of what one emits at all times.

When one is truly "looking out for number one,"
One is effectively looking out for all,
For there is no "other" to be separated from.
Thus the harmony of one's thoughts and actions,
Contribute to the perfect development of the universe.

When one's thoughts are purely love,
One does not exclude nor differentiate.

Love has no "likes" or "dislikes."

That perfect thought,
That perfect seed,
Not dependent upon life's circumstances.
For that perfect thought,
That perfect seed,

APHORISMS: FOR THOSE WHO SEEK
THE TRUTH

Is the Creator of all creation.

When one no longer chooses,
One is chosen.

When the blue sky is clearly seen,
Appreciate the blue sky.
When the clouds are present,
Appreciate the clouds.

It is not the circumstances of life that break or uplift one,
It is the interpretation one puts upon the circumstances.

One who moves beyond what one is taught,
Is comparable to one who has left one's native land.
One is sure to encounter new experiences along the way.

All answers lie where the questions originate.

Many souls,
Only one source.
Many cells,
Only one body.
Many thoughts,
Only one mind.

Without harmony,
There's no movement.
The actions of one who is anchored to a particular desire,
Should not be taken personally by one who is free of such
        desire.

The same urge that motivates one to be enslaved,
Is the same urge that frees oneself.
A conscious being <u>knows</u> the two hungers are really one.

Fear can easily be traced back to its origin;
All one has to do is look within.

If the seed of fear is planted in one's mind,
Then the object of that fear appears menacing,
And all events henceforth are interpreted according to that
        fear.

Anything which is worth learning comes directly from
        experience,
And all that is not worth learning is stored in books.
Books only stimulate the thoughts within,
Which draw from the experiences of one's self.

That which appears "positive" or "negative" at the time,
Serves as an opportunity to strengthen one's self.

One must become adaptable like water,
And take the shape of the container—the present moment.

To truly be encouraged,
One must take a journey within.
There one will find the seed of Perfection.
That which is perfect,
Needs no correction or adjustment.
By focusing on the "goal,"
One forgets the process.

The point is not what one has done,

APHORISMS: FOR THOSE WHO SEEK THE TRUTH

Or what one will do,
But what one is doing.

One can not modify what is.

Wherever one steps,
The Path appears beneath one's feet.

Agitation and suffering originate from within,
So can peace!

One does not need to "kill" the desires,
Only starve them to death.

If one feeds a cat,
It will keep coming around.
Stop feeding it,
And eventually it will not bother to come around any more.
Likewise it is so with desires.

Why...? Stop right there!
Any thing further is fruitless.

One ever watchful and alert creates no excuse.

If "likes" and "dislikes" were real,
Every one would have the same "likes" and "dislikes."
Various cultivations result in various cultures.

The best way to be "unselfish,"
Is to concentrate on one's self.

The Perfect Seed is the employment of the mind as a
      mirror:
It grasps nothing and refuses nothing.
It receives an image,
But it does not keep it.

When a question surfaces from within the questioner,
The questioner must also look within for the answer.

The so-called living are full of doubt and questions.
In order to truly be alive,
One's mind must become quiet and reposed,
Just like the residents of a graveyard.

Seasoning was designed to enhance the flavor of food.
Experiences occur in order to enhance one's life.

In the Supreme Consciousness,
All things are perfect and well-ordered.
Those who align and attune themselves to this reality,
So do they become perfect.

One who knows oneself,
Is among the wisest in the world.
One's action is a shadow of one's thought,
Which is a product of one's mind,
And the "three" are in harmony.

APHORISMS: FOR THOSE WHO SEEK THE TRUTH

CHAPTER 7: THE FALLEN LEAF

The fallen leaf,
No longer attached to a branch.
It appears lifeless and helpless,
Listlessly blowing in the wind.
But it is really alive and evolving,
Undergoing metamorphosis even in seeming death,
Thus being conducive to its atmosphere.

So it is with the mind:
No longer attached to concepts and beliefs and ideals,
It appeas dull and defenseless,
Swayed by the influences without.
But it is eally powerful and causative,
Undergoing development even during—seemingly—
        inaction,
Thus being free to creat.

The fallen leaf,
When in the midst of many other leaves blowing in the
        wind,
Is indistinguishable to the naked eye from afar.

So it is with a thought.
When in the midst of many other thoughts flowing in the
        mind,
It is impersonal to the conscious mind which sees things
        objectively.

On who has accumulated an abundance of material wealth,

"Peace is not the absence of trials and tribulations, but the absence of doubt and confusion." –Asitis Now

Leaves most of it at home while traveling on a journey.

The more one looks out of one's window at the world,
The more one forgets who the "observer" is.

Before one ascends,
One must first descend.

One must consciously plumb the depths of the unconscious.
This is what is meant by the saying, "to be conscious."

The fallen leaf is forever associated with t tree it fell from.
One's mind is forever associated with the experiences one
        undergoes.

When one travels into an unknown world,
The experience of this terrain is a disconnecting encounter,
For the one who thinks one knows is oneself.

Ignorance of one's true nature,
Is the real source of conflict.

One who studies a fallen leaf,
Knows the tree it fell from.
And one who journeys inwardly,
Knows the origin of all "things."

One cannot give birth to consciousness,
Without first going through the labor pains.

To the so-called "rational,"
I Am Contradictory.

APHORISMS: FOR THOSE WHO SEEK THE TRUTH

Even that which is "waste,"
Is conducive to growth.

The answer lies where the questions arise.

When one's mind is "made up,"
The ears become clogged.

When one is driven by desires,
One's vision becomes cloudy and distorted.

Physical hunger is an experience one should be willing to
      explore.

One is a product of one's influences.

All of the "differences" between people,
Are like the ingredients one puts in a cake.
The taste is dependent upon the elements included.

Every existent is compounded by causes and conditions,
And is void of an independent self.

There's no one to thank.
There's no "me" to thank.
There's no "you" to thank.
Thank the Cosmos.

Pain is <u>not</u> one's enemy.
One's biggest enemy is resistance to it.

When the time comes for the fallen leaf to detach itself,

"Peace is not the absence of trials and tribulations, but the absence of doubt and confusion." –Asitis Now

From the tree which brought forth it,
The fallen leaf simply detaches itself.

Likewise, when the time comes for the mind to free itself,
From the conditions and experiences which influenced it,
The mind simply becomes free.

Many find fault with the seasons,
Dependent upon perceptions.
Is it any wonder that "they" would find fault with each
          "other?"

When one is doing what one is called to do,
There is no need or desire to go on a vacation.

Whether in vibrancy or decay,
The fallen leaf is still the same leaf.

Whether positive or negative,
It is the same energy force that creates the manifestation.

If one loves comfort and convenience,
One is a slave to them both.

To <u>Truly</u> live in the Now,
Is to be present consciously in the action.

During the "Fall" season,
Fallen leaves are of commonplace appearances.
Flawless in nature without being conspicuous.
Poignant without having to be "pretty."
So true they do not have to be "real."
Comprehensive rather than known.

68

APHORISMS: FOR THOSE WHO SEEK THE TRUTH

Tranquil without passivity.
Being without becoming.
Authoritative without being dominant.
So it is with Pure Mind.

One does not achieve Pure Mind,
One dis-covers it.

To arrive at simplicity,
One must pass through knowledge.

One who is not firmly fixed in mind,
Is diverted by various types of fruitive acts.

One who is Governor of self,
Is ungoverned by "others."

One who "needs a break,"
Is one who breaks from reality,
For there is no "breaking away."

The mind is forever associated with the thoughts it
        conceives.

Just as a cashier counts millions of dollars for his employer,
Never claiming the money as one's own,
So it is with one who has attained supreme awareness,
Never claiming ownership of material and temporal things.

One who has "friends,"
Separates oneself from Me.

When one becomes "intimate" with "another one,"
Through the "sharing of minds,"
One slams the door on pure enlightenment.
It is through observation of one another's manifestative
      qualities,
That one truly becomes enlightened.

One who ceases excessive talking,
Enters into Being.

Chaos is that realm of thoughts,
Before one makes a choice to do or say <u>any</u> thing.

Silence makes the restless nervous.

The mind is both friend and foe.
Perception is the key to this realization.

The mind is the cause of bondage,
And the mind is the cause of liberation.

For one who has conquered the mind,
It is the best of friends.
But for one who has failed to do so,
It is the greatest of enemies.

It is the mind that one must respect,
Not the "man."

So many fallen leaves,
But so little trees.
So many chaotic thoughts,
But so little deeds.

APHORISMS: FOR THOSE WHO SEEK THE TRUTH

Answers are expected,
Even when they aren't necessary.

To hope is to expect.
To expect is to predict.
To predict is to project.
To project is to envision.
To envision is to see.
To see is to experience.
Thus: If experience is to be the ultimate,
Why waste energy on the lesser activities.

The solution has always been in existence,
It is the problem that is newly created.

Once the veil is removed,
Once can never "re-veal."

Those who are rash in speculation,
Are akin to those who wander aimlessly in the world.
Though there are any places to go,
There is no precise place to be.

A demon's action is a reflection of a nomad's thoughts.

How does one move?
Step by step.

Thought is a weapon one uses to attack or defend.
Thought is the tool by which one makes a choice.
Thought sets one's purpose and the way to reach it.

Trying to grasp thoughts in the mind,
Is comparable to chasing leaves in a storm.

To cling to words is to embrace definition,
And to embrace definition is to set limitations.

What is death and decay to the masses,
Is natural growth to Me.

To love a thing is to know and love its nature.

The power to achieve or to destroy one's happiness,
Lies within oneself.

When one does not seek or need external approval,
One is most powerful.

Both limitations and liberations are aspects of me.

One need not a "preacher" to dispense reality.
Reality alone is capable of transmitting its message.

One must not only be conscious of Me,
One must be <u>actively</u> conscious of Me.

When one seeks happiness,
One confesses that one's present state is not happy enough.

In trying to bring happiness to others,
One brings about unhappiness in one's self.
In trying to appease the mind of others,
One dams the flow of creativity in one's self.

APHORISMS: FOR THOSE WHO SEEK THE TRUTH

In trying <u>not</u> to hurt the feelings of others,
One's own feelings become subordinate.

In Autumn the leaves fall from the tree.
In winter the tree is barren.
In spring new leaves grow and replace the fallen ones.
In summer the new leaves prepare to follow the way of the
       old ones.
This is also the process of the mind.

Truth is manifested through pressure.

One who avoids challenges will never know transcendence.

External stimulation leads to internal depression,
When one <u>no</u> <u>longer</u> has the external means to achieve the
       end.

Mood swings are the product of the monkey mind.

That which is <u>without</u> cannot enter <u>within.</u>
Only the wish and desire <u>within</u> for that which is <u>without</u>
Suffuses one's whole being; thereby discontentment is
       aroused from its slumber.

It is the fallen leaf which naturally is detached from the tree
which bore it that truly experiences liberty.

The seasons of life reflect the Unchanging Law of Changes.

CHAPTER 8: A MOTH ON THE WALL

What patience a moth exhibits,
By being totally still on the wall.
Is it asleep?
Is it meditating?
Or is it simply being observant?
Regardless of the answer,
A moth does what a moth does.
Questions are not befitting of a moth.

The best companion one could have <u>is</u> solitude.

<u>Fate</u> is the result of feat.

One who is unhappy can not cultivate happiness within
others.

One truly transcends influences when one laughs at
nothing.

In order to be as invisible as a moth on the wall,
One must veil one's innermost thoughts.

In being, one is flowing with thought.
In thinking, one is not flowing with being.

For every individual who flees for refuge into the crowd,
And so flees in cowardice from being an individual,
Such a one contributes his share of cowardliness to the
cowardliness which is known as the "crowd."
Ignorance is <u>not</u> bliss.
Ignorance <u>is</u> ignorant!

74

APHORISMS: FOR THOSE WHO SEEK THE TRUTH

Enemies can look like friends,
And friends could look like enemies.

Reality is fundamentally agreement.
What is agreed upon to be real is real.

One who learns the reality of facing life experiences,
Does so when one finds one's self in solitude.

A lie has no problem getting a ride,
But I catch hell trying to hitchhike.

When one makes a conscious choice to live in the Now,
One does not want any thing for nothing;
Least of all life.

It is through experience that one realizes,
That struggle produces strength,
And the more one embraces strife,
The more powerful one is.

Hope is the worst of delusions,
Since it prolongs the torment through anticipation.

One who sleeps soundly,
Is one whose life lacks inner significance.

The difference between a "winner" and a "whiner,"
Is the sound of the "I."

Neutrality helps the oppressor,

"Peace is not the absence of trials and tribulations, but the absence of doubt and confusion." –Asitis Now

Never the victim.
Silence encourages the tormentor,
Never the tormented.

Religion is for people who are afraid of going to hell;
Spirituality is for those who have been there.

Words are the great foes of reality.

Follow those who search for Me,
And run from those who say they have found Me.

Answers to the big questions in life,
Have got to come from within.

Creation is an act of will.

The day one admits being immature,
Is the day one becomes wise.

Two things one can't do perfectly: Good and bad.

Seeing first one's own immaturity is humility;
The fruit of that vision is tolerance.

Reality is perception;
Perception changes;
Reality is fluid.

It is easier for one to be truthful with another,
Than it is for one to be truthful with one's own self.

Fear is that darkroom where negatives are developed.

APHORISMS: FOR THOSE WHO SEEK THE TRUTH

Don't hate! Innovate!

One need not <u>more</u> information to be creative,
But rather new and different ways of thinking
About the information that one already has.

One with unrestrained imagination,
Is conscious of all fate,
Thereby one's happiness waits patiently for the call.

To pray is to be creative.
Prayer is creativity.

Even in your indecisions,
You have made decisions.

Is it a coincidence that <u>belief</u> <u>systems</u>
Have the same initials as <u>bull</u> <u>shit</u>?

Man is not the creature of circumstances.
Circumstances are the creatures of men.

Decisions—not conditions—determine destiny.

If you choose unconsciously,
You evolve unconsciously.
If you choose consciously,
You evolve consciously.

What the masses call "mistakes,"
I call experiences.

"Peace is not the absence of trials and tribulations, but the absence of doubt and confusion." –Asitis Now

Madmen never doubt their sanity.

Death lies on the surface.
In order to find life,
One must go beneath the surface,
For there exists reproduction.

The Present only has a being in nature.
Things Past have a being in memory.
Things to come have no being at all.

Do or do not; there is no try.

If you want to know who your enemy is,
Take a look at the fabricated persona within.

What else is human nature but a emphemism for inertia,
A cultural conditioning,
And what one is before making something of one's self?
One's so-called human nature,
Is precisely what one should do well to overcome.

In looking at life as it is,
One will easily see what it is not.

There is no such thing as perpetual tranquility
Of mind on this plane,
Because life itself is but motion.
The moment one is no longer certain of "the future,"
Is the moment one becomes free to explore life itself.

Just as one moth's nature is in harmony with another's,

APHORISMS: FOR THOSE WHO SEEK THE TRUTH

So do all humanity drink from the same river of emotions.

There is no such entity as perfect isolation.

Every moment of one's existence,
Is to be regarded with reflection and curiosity,
Every moment of one's existence,
Is a lesson within a lesson.

A scientist has more failures than success,
And when success finally does manifest itself,
The scientist goes out and fails some more.

Though "two" may start at opposite poles,
As long as they both continuously move forward,
They will eventually end up in the same position.

It's good to suffer,
Don't complain.
Bear, bow, accept, and be grateful that you suffer.
For in this you become stronger than those who are
laughing,
And happy.

Every thing "bad" comes from the mind,
Because the mind asks too many questions.

There are two types of people who are reliant,
Those who believe and those who know.
Those who believe rely on others' experiences,
And those who know rely on their own.

"Idle" is a variation of the word "lied."

When one dis covers an other's dislikes,
One dis covers an other's weaknesses.

To search for Me is to lack Me,
And to quest for love is to be devoid of it.

Hu Man in expression,
But divine in creation,
And limitless in potentiality.

The Hu Man's divine nature,
Is buried deep within the earth.

All dis covery is self-discovery.
All knowledge is self-knowledge.

How does one study the mind?
Through introspection and self-contemplation.

"Self-Reverence...Self-Knowledge...Self-Control,
These three alone lead life to sovereign power."

One may not be able to prevent birds from flying
Over one's head,
But one has a right to determine whether they
Shall make nests in his hair.
The seed of an unripe fruit,
Clings tenaciously to the flesh,
While the seed of a ripe fruit,
Falls out with no particle of flesh clinging to it.

APHORISMS: FOR THOSE WHO SEEK THE TRUTH

Control your roll,
And gauge your stage.

The purpose of life is not happiness,
But experience.
Sorrow and pain are one's most benevolent leaders,
While the joys of life are but fleeting.

Experience is knowledge of the effects which follow acts.

The course that one runs,
Is based upon one's vision.

Each action—even the smallest,
Is pregnant with consequences.

The coward resides within a crowd.

Be sure of one thing: No thing is sure.

As one blossoms, old things pass away.

It isn't the getting that gives,
But the giving that gets.

There is no moderation with love.

Believing in beliefs is like seasoning the air.
All must journey: Whether one does so in awareness,
Or in ignorance, determines the destination.

Each moment is a moment of chance.

"Peace is not the absence of trials and tribulations, but the absence of doubt and confusion." –Asitis Now

Whatever one does in that moment is relvant to one's self.

Just as the <u>physically</u> dead do not heal,
Neither can they who are "dead" to the knowledge of self.

To the enlightened, one's best friend is one's self,
And one's worst enemy is one's self.
It's all a matter of perception.

A moth on the wall does not need confirmation
That it is a moth on the wall.
Neither does one who exercises willpower and discipline.

CHAPTER 9: A BLAZING FIRE

A blazing fire is capable of both destruction and purification.
So, it is with the mind.

No matter where one goes,
One must still deal with one's self.

When you begin to see the world around you, and within
you,
As a teacher, then you have learned a most valuable lesson.

One, who is inspired by experiences and <u>not knowing</u>
Doesn't "believe" in beliefs.
And, one too busy exploring the present,
Doesn't have time for hope.

Speculation about possibilities,
Only brings about more speculation.

Since "perfect" <u>originally</u> meant "To do completely,"
Every physical deed is perfect.

One who has friends has enemies,
Thus one is biased.

The conscience is Guide.
The Mind is Guide.

A true master of one's self

Is like an eagle which flies through the sky.
Both leave no footprints to follow.

One who has "loved ones" has unloved ones,
Thus one is prejudiced.

Reality is the moment of experience
<u>Before </u>the intellectualization takes place.

The past exists only in one's memories,
The future only in one's plans.
The present is one's only reality.

One who owes has woes.

One who is drawn to determine,
Is one who is conditioned to deter mind.

It is the mind that influences,
Not the object of interest or circumstance.

Life is "softness" and flexibility,
Death is rigidity and inflexibility.
Those who are flexible in their thinking are <u>alive</u>,
And those who are rigid in their beliefs are <u>dead</u>.

The natural inclination is to be drawn to pain<u>less</u>
        experiences.
The natural way is that—some times—painful experiences
Will be drawn to you.

The invisible begs the visible,

APHORISMS: FOR THOSE WHO SEEK THE TRUTH

Thereby the moment precedes the "Now."

Happiness and sadness both arise from the same source;
They only patiently await their turn to reign.

Conceived—Birthed—Lived—Died:
These four can be attributed to the four seasons of life.

No-am in one's mind produces the mo-an in one's life.

The king of Now is K-Now-Ing.
However, it is Not K-Now-Ing that spurs one on to become
King in the first place.

To the skeptic: "Seeing is believing."
To the experiencer: Seeing is seeing.

To the one what is considered "Hu man,"
The evacuation of one's bowels, is universal.

"Perfection" and "Imperfection"—in reality—
Are only words.
Life itself needs no labels or definitions.

Just as one who chases one's own shadow
Will run endlessly,
So it is with one who pursues knowledge.

To the clinger: Justice is an art that benefits friends
And injures enemies.

To pursue one's own interests is in accord with nature.

"Peace is not the absence of trials and tribulations, but the absence of doubt and confusion." –Asitis Now

---

One who stays rooted in the familiar learns no thing.

The moment one journeys into the realm of opinions
Is the moment one departs from reality.

The mind is the "creator" of experiences
Via interest in actualities.

That which is capable of existing,
But not yet existing,
Exists in the loins of man.

When beneficial: True leaders break all rules,
Including their own.

Reality includes every viewpoint.

I come when one experiences without analyzation.

Thinking thought is finite, visible, limited.
Being thought is infinite, invisible, unlimited.

Just because one is confused about one's own life,
Doesn't mean that one's own life is confused.

When one enjoys what one is doing,
One is being one's best.

"Evil" pertains to the dead things—unproductivity,
And is a direct reversal to the "live" things—productivity.
However..."both" are really a "veil."
Ideas are born and they die.
Thus...the truly enlightened are not attached to them.

APHORISMS: FOR THOSE WHO SEEK THE TRUTH

One mired in opinions enjoys the illusion of being clean.

"Genius" accepts "genius" unconditionally.

One thing is certain: There is no thing certain.

"Let the dead bury the dead" is synonymous to "Let the deed replace the deed," which is synonymous to "Let the action absorb the action, which is (still) synonymous to "Let the Now continue and the 'past' die."

A perfect diamond is diamond left in its natural state.

What you love is your god. What you live is your guide.

Two things hinder one in expressing one's self fully: Misdirected drives and undesirable tradition.

Having attained a state of awareness one knows intuitively that what one is is not what one can become.

"Great spirits have always encountered violent opposition from mediocre minds."

Be grateful to all those people who said "no" to you. It is because of them one does for one's self.

"It is a simple procedure to calculate the number of seeds in an apple. But who among you can ever say how many apples are in a seed?"

Death is passive. She awaits all who live. Those who live life fully long to feel her embrace because they know they will surely enter into her arms.

Interpretations of reality are interpretations of reality. Reality is reality. It needs no interpretation. It only needs to be experienced.

"Society" says the "cost of living has gone up." I say the greed of mankind has increased.

Circumstances do not make one what one is. They reveal what one has chosen to be.

One is the sum total of one's choices.

The human in being is a cocktail of nature and nurture.

Evil is the veil that keeps one from knowing how to live in the moment.

Moving from the personal to the universal allows one to be spontaneous, creative, and innovative.

One can't have intimacy without honesty.

"Thinking is the great enemy of perfection."
"The human mind, once stretched to a new idea, never goes back to its original dimension."

"Making" love is out of the question, since it already exists. Recognizing love is the key to inner peace.

APHORISMS: FOR THOSE WHO SEEK THE TRUTH

To "own it" is to "<u>now</u> it."

Arguing with reality is akin to arguing with a doorknob. When all is expressed, those things will still be those things.

Just as a shadow is a shadow until light is shed on it, So it is with one who mimics an other. The moment the light of consciousness is shed upon a mimic is the moment when the mimic disappears.

Actuality is complete and perfect. Potentiality has the capability of being perfected.

CHAPTER 10: BURYING THE DEAD

When your struggles with ME cease to exist, and your desire to memorialize your deeds are unceremoniously entombed, <u>doing</u> and <u>being</u> are no longer entangled words and <u>I</u> am easily recognizable in the midst of everything.

It is I who holds the key to facing ME. When you become entranced with your actions and conversations, you are in love with you and <u>not</u> ME. Complaining is the offspring of dead deeds, and worrying is the fruit of dead deeds anticipated. The more you imagine yourself to be filled with ME, the more you become unimaginative; and the more unimaginative you become, the more I am kept at bay in <u>your</u> mind.

When you find yourself face to face with an epiphany you see tiny glimpses of ME. By the time you make an attempt to memorialize ME through description you become confused, disoriented, and counted a fool. Embrace the epiphany without clinging to it, and you will have more time to spend in My company and no need to describe ME, for I AM without description, and I AM always in your immediate vicinity.

Trying to find ME in your mind is akin to ice skating on an ocean. The only reward you will receive for your

APHORISMS: FOR THOSE WHO SEEK THE TRUTH

efforts is death by drowning in a sea of thoughts. I do not die, nor am I capable of being slain. I AM not a concept produced by the mind, nor am I crafted by "gifted hands." I AM both the creator and the destroyer of all that exists. If you dare to dream of pursuing ME I will crush your dreams. If you make plans to share ME with others, you will <u>dis cover</u> that you cannot distribute ME in portions or small pieces for I AM whole. I cannot be shared, and I will never be distributed in any form or fashion. I AM the maker of forms and I do the fashioning. It is I who buries deeds and I who brings to life what can never be predicted by the human intellect.

Remember ME always and your life is filled with focus. Revisit the tomb of past deeds and speeches and your life is filled with distractions. Just as a resurrected zombie is consumed with thoughts of <u>flesh,</u> so is one whose mind is consumed with thoughts of <u>self</u>-satisfaction. They both are controlled by uncontrollable lust. One who unearths the past only succeeds in exploring dead things. One who unearths the present is extremely surprised by what he finds: ME!

I AM incorrectly named by many who believe they have a handle on ME, but it is I who has a handle on them. They pass their ideologies on to you and become self-satisfied that they have accomplished something, but when I am revealed to them in the rawest of forms, they being to lose cohesiveness and their ideologies die along with them.

When you find <u>yourself</u> motivated by ME you will <u>dis cover</u> more aspects of ME, and the more aspects of ME you encounter, the more I will teach you that there are no boundaries when it comes to learning all about ME. Only when you begin to become enchanted by <u>your</u> very own <u>dis coveries</u> do you become motivated by your very own desires, and your desires only lead to frustration and spiritual death. There I <u>do not</u> live!

I only hurt those who do not love ME. If you seek ME on a daily basis you are never injured by MY revelations, for you are not afraid to face ME. Belief and I are in no way related or interrelated, although belief is often mistaken for ME by the religious mentality. Belief is a product of a deluded mind, and it is I that the deluded one appears to be seeking. However, because of the "belief" that one knows ME one is, in fact, far from the knowledge of ME, because I AM always right there in their presence even though they do not <u>acknowledge</u> ME.

I AM always with you. I will never leave you. Although you may, sometimes, depart from ME through your beliefs and traditions and look for ME "elsewhere," I AM still your eternal companion. People run from ME not because I am scary but because they are afraid of letting go of their beliefs. They are more comfortable with a lie than they are with ME.

What am I? Can you find ME in your ancient scriptures? Can you capture ME in a jar? Do you look for ME IN the sky? Can you define ME with your words? Do I belong to a particular culture? Do I dwell with a certain type of person? Can you wish for ME? Can you pray ME into existence? Can you pray ME out of existence? All of these questions, and more, seem to be associates of MINE; however, these sorts of questions only produce more questions.

When a human limb is found to be gangrenous, the optimum solution is to amputate the limb before the poison spreads to the rest of the body. So it is with painful memories and hurtful disappointments. The sooner you excise the decayed memory from your mind, the sooner the healing stage can begin and natural growth, which brings forth full acceptance of <u>all</u> of life's experiences as they occur, makes it easier to see ME for what I <u>AM</u>.

If a past deed perpetrated against you still stirs up anger within you when you recall it, then it is safe to say that you haven't forgiven the offender for his or her trespass. When you become intimate with ME you will have no problem remembering the deed while, simultaneously, expressing empathy with the offender <u>and</u> forgiving them, because you <u>know</u> that you are perfectly capable of offending someone in the same manner as they have offended you.

When you hold onto beliefs without exhausting all of the other possibilities the chances of your mind being renewed by MY revelations are as possible as a butterfly becoming a caterpillar again. I do not reveal MYSELF to those who are blind.

When you are tempted to "believe" that you are "superior" or "better" than someone else I will remind you every time that you are on the toilet evacuating your bowels that you are not. At that time I will look you directly in the eyes and reveal MYSELF to you. Althou you may attempt to shut them immediately, trying to block ME out, it will be too late, because you cannot erase ME from your mind.

If you decide to live off a diet of only salt; no food, no water, no other nutrients, and so forth, you will eventually die from malnutrition, because salt by itself is not enough to keep you alive. Although it is good for seasoning your food and making it taste "better," it is not essential that you have it in every meal. So it is with trying to live off of the memory of "better times" and pleasurable moments. Although the memories might make you feel all warm and fuzzy inside it will <u>not</u> sustain you in your present condition <u>nor</u> create a more prosperous lifestyle for you in your "future."

If you live your life fully in ME you will never live unrealistically ever again. I will guide you in everything. All that is required of you is that you stop clinging to your past and let your present life be all the influence you will ever need in order to live. Now go and "Let the dead bury their dead..."

APHORISMS: FOR THOSE WHO SEEK THE TRUTH

THE BEGINNING ...

"Peace is not the absence of trials and tribulations, but the absence of doubt and confusion." –Asitis Now

ABOUT THE AUTHOR

Asitis Now is the spiritual, creative, inspired, intellectual alter ego of George Woods, a gifted author, scholar, and student of life.

Woods has always had a questioning nature and a thirst for knowledge. To this end, he is a voracious reader, devouring many great literary texts with all the hunger of a starving man. Using this acquired knowledge as a foundation, he analyzes what he has learned in the context of his vast life experience and expands his insights beyond the boundaries created by society. He is fluent in Hebrew, Greek, and Arabic and has completed extensive studies in the texts of major world religions and philosophies.

He resides in Atlanta, Georgia. He states that his primary purpose in life is to help others seeking self-enlightenment and mental freedom.

For more on this author and his work, visit nowledgecommunications.webs.com .

"Peace is not the absence of trials and tribulations, but the absence of doubt and confusion." **-Asitis Now**

APHORISMS: FOR THOSE WHO SEEK THE TRUTH

OTHER WORKS BY ASITIS NOW

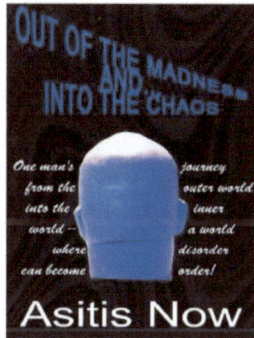

GROW INTO THE FULLNESS OF ALL THAT YOU ARE DESTINED TO BE ... AND BEYOND!

Has modern-day religion left you frustrated, disillusioned, and seeking answers?

Are you seeking a deeper meaning of life and your inner self?

Do you sometimes feel that you and the rest of the world are out of sync, that you view everything around you from the perspective of an eagle's-eye view while others are bound to the ground?

Do you desire to tap into your Higher Power and drink of the fountain of greatness?

"Peace is not the absence of trials and tribulations, but the absence of doubt and confusion." –Asitis Now

---

If you answered yes to any of the above, then **Out of the Madness and Into the Chaos** is written just for you. **Out of the Madness and Into the Chaos** is an intellectual treatise of one man's journey into the deeper spiritual recesses of himself. Using his own personal experiences and newfound revelations and insights, the author gives a new and unique perspective on how one can create order from the disorder of inner turmoil and thereby live a better life. This is a book of self-discovery that follows a spiritual pathway rather than the conventional religious road, and enlightenment is the pot of gold found at the end of the rainbow.

Imprison a weak mind in a cage,

Through boredom, it will revert back to its primitive past and mimic a caged animal.

Imprison a powerful mind in a cage,

Through creativity, it will become advanced in its infinite present and free itself from the confines of its self-imposed cage of limitations.

– Asitis Now

"Peace is not the absence of trials and tribulations, but the absence of doubt and confusion." –Asitis Now